Spell Well!

by **Dee Benscoter and Geri Harris**

S C H O L A S T I C
PROFESSIONAL**B**OOKS

New York • Toronto • London • Auckland • Sydney
Mexico City • New Delhi • Hong Kong

Dedication

To our families who encouraged us
and had faith in our ideas.
And, to best friends—who work
so well together.

Cover design by Norma Ortiz
Interior design by Sydney Wright

ISBN: 0-439-18519-X

Contents

Contents (cont.)

❋ Spelling Practice Activities ❋

❋ Spelling Contracts ❋

Introduction

"Spelling is boring!"

"I hate spelling!"

"Why do we always have to do the same things every week?"

Do these words sound familiar? They do to us! Over the many years that we have been teaching, we have heard our students make statements like those above. Spelling is one of the skills that we, as teachers, expect our students to practice. We give them the rules, demonstrate usage with examples, and try to create innovative ways for students to practice their spelling lists.

Yet, as many of us know, students dread spelling practice and find the drills mundane and tiring. The goal of this book is to provide students with alternative spelling activities, activities that they *want* to do. As an unexpected bonus, we've also discovered that these activities motivate reluctant writers. As they complete the activities in this book, your students will

* experience new ways to practice spelling words;
* develop a better understanding of each word's meaning;
* hone writing skills;
* see both spelling and vocabulary as part of daily life, not just another half-hour assignment;
* experience new dimensions in higher-level thinking skills.

The activities are divided into two types. Those under **Spelling Activities That Build Vocabulary** require students to know the word meaning and be able to use a dictionary or a thesaurus. Those listed under **Spelling Practice Activities** are drill activities. In addition, many of the activities also provide students with opportunities to work in cooperative groups.

In this book, you will also find several activity sheets for contracts. We have found these sheets helpful for students who have alternate word lists. They encourage students to have fun as they plan their own practice activities.

Feel free to incorporate the activities into your regular spelling program as alternative lessons, or introduce the activities for additional practice. For students who readily learn the weekly list, these activities can serve as practice for independent word lists.

We hope that your students will have as much fun as ours have had using these lessons. Happy spelling, and spell well!

Letter Mania

As a way to demonstrate to students the importance of spelling well, invite them to incorporate their spelling words in a real-world writing activity—letter writing. While students write letters to partners, they will be practicing and learning their spelling words.

1. Have students work in pairs.

2. Direct each student to write a friendly letter to his or her partner using all the spelling words.

3. Ask the letter writers to underline each spelling word.

4. Hold the letters until the following week. At that time, pass them out to the students to whom they were written.

5. After reading the letters, encourage the partners to answer them, using the spelling words for the current week.

> Dear carefree Matt,
>
> How are you doing? I am fine. Wherever have you been? Were you at Skateland with somebody? This weekend I slept outside with my grandparents. My grandfather gave me a haircut while we listened to my favorite music group, No One, on my new tape recorder.
> Do you know my friend who is taking a sign language class? She was running into the courthouse where her sign language class was held when she fell, because she got a side effect that was caused by her medicine. Everybody saw it happen, so they rushed her to the hospital that looks like a sky scraper. They put her in one of those polka dot night gowns. Her sign language teacher brought everybody in her class to see her in the hospital. They brought her everything she could possibly need. Once everyone had left, she said something fell on her from nowhere. It gave her a feeling that her health was at a dead end, and she was never going to improve. Well, I have to go.
>
> Your forever friend,
>
> Kristi
>
> PS I hope you got 100% on your quiz over the solar system!

Variations

For other letter-writing activities using the spelling words, suggest that students

* write a business letter explaining a problem they had with an item they purchased;
* answer an ad from the classified section of the newspaper;
* write a letter of recommendation for someone;
* create greeting cards with messages for a holiday or special occasion.

Poem Fun

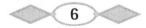

Writing poetry is an excellent way for students to reinforce their understanding of new vocabulary and practice spelling their words. It also gives students an opportunity to use words in imaginative ways.

1 Start by offering students a choice of poetry styles. For example:

> ### Forms of Poetry
>
> **Acrostic**—a poem that uses each letter of a word for the first line.
>
> **Couplet** (ideal for homophones)—two lines that end with rhyming words.
>
> **Tongue Twister** (ideal for working with prefixes)—sentences with words that have the same beginning sounds.
>
> **Haiku**—a three-line poem that has five syllables in the first line; seven syllables in the second line; and five syllables in the last line.
>
> **Cinquain**—a five-line poem. The first and last lines are the same word; the second line has two adjectives that describe the word, the third line has three verbs that describe the word, the fourth line is a simile related to the word.
>
> **Diamante**—(ideal for antonyms) a seven-line poem that forms a diamond shape. The first and last line are the antonyms, the second and sixth lines have two adjectives each that tell about the antonym closest to it, the third and fifth lines have three verbs for each, and the fourth line provides four nouns (two for the first antonym and two for the following antonym).
>
> **Simile**—a comparison using the words *like* or *as.*
>
> **Metaphor**—a direct comparison, not using the words *like* or *as.*

2 Have your students select a small set of the words and choose a poetry form. Invite students to write several poems and experiment with several forms so they use all their spelling words.

3 When the poems are complete, have students display them in creative ways. For example, have them

- draw illustrations to go with the poems;
- make banners or posters for the poems;
- share the poems with friends in the classroom;
- frame the poems for display;
- write the poems on adding-machine tape, then roll up the tape, tie it with a ribbon, and give the poem to a friend;
- decorate paper lunch bags with the poems, then bring their lunches to school in them;
- decorate covers for a textbook of favorite poems;

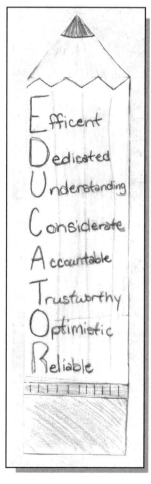

Cartoon Strips

Just as kids love to read cartoon strips, they also enjoy creating their own. In this activity, students use their weekly spelling list to create the dialogue for one or two cartoon strips.

1 Review with students the components of a cartoon strip and what makes a cartoon strip different from other types of reading material, such as its individual panels and the dialogue shown in speech bubbles.

2 Reproduce and pass out the cartoon-strip pattern on page 9. Give each student at least two copies. Remind students to be sure they understand the meanings of the words they choose to use.

3 Encourage students to consider situations in which characters would say many of the spelling words. Listed below are some ideas for students to consider.

- Lunchtime in the cafeteria
- Walking to school
- Forgetting to bring back their school work
- Playing a sport
- Trying to decide on a movie to rent
- Planning or attending a party
- Winning the big game
- Falling in love
- A trip to the mall
- Running for a school office

- Talking a parent into letting them do something
- A science experiment that went wrong
- Sneaking a new pet into the home
- Convincing a friend to share something
- Being late for school or the bus
- Falling asleep in class
- Passing a note in class
- Their first music program at school, or going to the concert of a favorite band

Cartoon Strip

Create your own cartoon strip in the squares below. Your spelling words can be part of the dialogue; names of places, people, things; or a character's thoughts. Underline each spelling word. Be creative and have fun!

Title of Your Cartoon Strip: _____

Fortune-Cookie Fun

If students have ever opened a fortune cookie, they know that they are greeted by wise words and sayings. Let students enlighten their classmates as they offer advice and predict futures for their friends with this fortune-cookie spelling activity.

1 First, talk with students about the purpose of fortune cookies and the paper slips inside. Invite students who recall such fortunes to share them with the class. If possible, you might have some fortune cookies on hand for volunteers to open and read the messages inside.

2 Ask students to write fortunes for their friends similar to those found in fortune cookies. Challenge them to include their spelling words in each fortune.

3 If time, resources, and interest allow, let students make fortune cookies out of modeling clay. Have them write their fortunes on small slips of paper, then fold the slips inside the clay cookies. Collect all the cookies. Then distribute them randomly so students can read the fortunes inside.

> 1. Football, There will be no _addition_ in yards.
> 2. Parents, You will have no _correction_ in my work.
> 3. Teacher, There will be no _complication_ to _multiplication_.
> 4. Operator, Your conversations will be short.
> 5. Scientist, You will have one bone in your bone _collection_.
> 6. Scientist, You will need more _information_ to see this situation.

Your mistakes will be brought to a HALT!

Punny Spelling

Puns are humorous plays on words for which the writer and reader must understand the words' meanings. Tom Swiftys are an excellent type of pun, for they require a good understanding of meanings and synonyms.

1 Have students review their spelling words and make a list of synonyms for each.

2 Challenge students to use a spelling word and one of the synonyms in a Tom Swifty.

3 Have students underline the spelling word and the synonym.

Samples of Tom Swiftys

"Turn off the <u>noisy</u> radio!" said Tom <u>loudly</u>.

"I made a big <u>error</u>," said Tom <u>mistakenly</u>.

"I will <u>tidy</u> up the house," said Tom <u>neatly</u>.

Conversation Frolic

This activity builds upon students' seemingly unquenchable need to talk and write notes in class. Why not give them the chance to chat and practice their spelling words at the same time?

1 Have students work in pairs.

2 Invite each student to write a note to his or her partner that incorporates several spelling words. Tell students to keep track of each spelling word they use. Ask students to underline the spelling words.

3 Direct students to exchange notes and reply to each other. Explain that this time you would like their notes to include different spelling words.

4 Let students continue writing and passing notes to each other until each partner has used all the spelling words.

Compound-Word Teasers

The next time your spelling list includes compound words, let students create their own brainteasers for their friends to solve.

1 Review the definition of a compound, and have students identify those words that fit the definition from their spelling list.

2 Ask students to copy each compound word, and then to break the compound word apart into its two individual words. Have them write these two words as well.

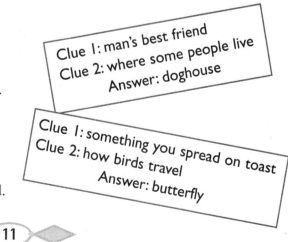

Clue 1: man's best friend
Clue 2: where some people live
Answer: doghouse

Clue 1: something you spread on toast
Clue 2: how birds travel
Answer: butterfly

3 Model how to write a definition or a clue for each of the individual words.

4 Have them put the two clues together for a friend to figure out the compound word.

Job Application

Completing a job application is a real-world skill that students will face at some time in their lives. Being able to express themselves and correctly spell words is essential for landing the job of their choice. Let your students practice not only their spelling words but this real-life skill as they complete this spelling activity.

1. Provide each student with a copy of the job application on pages 13 and 14. Review the application with the class.

2. Ask students to complete the form, encouraging them to use their spelling words. The words can be used for the names of people, schools, businesses, hobbies, past jobs, and so on. Make sure students understand that it doesn't matter if they've never actually held a job. This form is for practice only and the information can be creative.

3. Remind students that in the real world neatness and correct spelling are essential when filling out a job application.

4. Have students underline the spelling words.

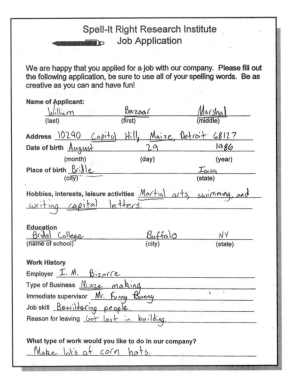

Spell-It Right Research Institute
Job Application

We are happy that you applied for a job with our company. Please fill out the following application, be sure to use all of your spelling words. Be as creative as you can and have fun!

Name of Applicant:
William   Bazaar   Marshal
(last)   (first)   (middle)

Address 10290 Capitol Hill, Maize, Detroit 68127
Date of birth August   29   1986
             (month)   (day)   (year)
Place of birth Bridle   Iowa
             (city)   (state)

Hobbies, interests, leisure activities Martial arts, swimming, and writing capital letters.

Education
Bridal College   Buffalo   NY
(name of school)   (city)   (state)

Work History
Employer I. M. Bizarre
Type of Business Maze making
Immediate supervisor Mr. Funny Bunny
Job skill Bewildering people.
Reason for leaving Got lost in building.

What type of work would you like to do in our company?
Make lots of corn hats.

Variations

* Ahead of time, obtain job applications from local fast-food restaurants or stores. Pass them out to the class, and encourage students to complete them.

* Cut out job listings from classified ads in the newspaper. Invite students to use their spelling words to write letters that explain why they would like to apply for a specific job.

Name _____   Date _____

Spell-It-Right Research Institute
Job Application

We are happy that you applied for a job with our company. Please fill out the following application. Be sure to use all of your spelling words. Be creative and have fun!

Name of Applicant

_____
(last)   (first)   (middle)

Address

_____

How long have you lived at this address?

_____

Previous address

_____

Date of birth   Place of birth

_____
(month)   (day)   (year)   (city)   (state)

Hobbies, interests, leisure activities

_____

_____

_____

_____

Education

_____
(school name)   (city)   (state)

_____
(school name)   (city)   (state)

Job Application (Continued)

Work History

Employer

_____

Type of business

_____

Immediate supervisor

_____

Job skill

_____

Reason for leaving

_____

Employer

_____

Type of business

_____

Immediate supervisor

_____

Job skill

_____

Reason for leaving

_____

What type of work would you like to do in our company?

_____

_____

_____

_____

Bumper Stickers

With their bright colors and catchy phrases, bumper stickers often intrigue students. And a bumper sticker's limited space means that writing must be concise and words used sparingly. Begin this activity by encouraging students to recall and describe some of the bumper stickers they've noticed that are funny, unique, or carry a special message. Once students have an opportunity to exchange ideas, they are often eager to create their own.

1. Ask students to brainstorm the topics or ideas that writers try to convey on bumper stickers. Have them choose an idea of their own.

2. Before they begin to write, instruct students to choose words from the spelling list that would work well to get across their bumper-sticker messages. (It may be that students only use a portion of their spelling-word list for this activity.)

3. Challenge students to write their bumper-sticker messages on writing paper. They should have at least two messages.

4. Provide each student with a copy of the bumper-sticker reproducible on page 16.

5. Have students write their catchy phrases within each bumper-sticker outline. Then encourage them to add pictures or colors to make the bumper stickers attractive.

6. Ask students to check their stickers for correct spelling and to underline each spelling word.

Variations

* Suggest that students write bumper-sticker slogans about your school or their favorite sports teams.

* Have them design the bumper stickers for classmates. Then challenge students to identify whom they are for.

* Invite students to write bumper stickers for famous historical figures, such as Abraham Lincoln, Thomas Edison, or Martin Luther King, Jr.

Bumper-Sticker Patterns

#10
My Secrets

"Want to know a secret?" What an intriguing way to begin a spelling lesson! People of all ages love to hear and tell secrets. This activity gives students the opportunity to make up secrets as they put their spelling words to use.

1. Invite students to share their own experiences with secrets. Was it easy or hard to keep the secret? When or how did the secret become public knowledge? Brainstorm ideas that secrets might be about.

2. Explain that you would like students to write a few secrets, using their spelling words. The secrets should be made up and totally outrageous. Emphasize that secrets should not be about anyone in school. In other words, you would like their writing to be as creative and inventive as possible.

3. After writing their secrets, have students underline the spelling words.

·Variations·

* Encourage students to write secrets that workers in a particular profession might write, such as a teacher, a mechanic, a fast-food worker, a musician, an actor, and so on.

* Suggest that students write secrets from an alien who is sending messages back to its planet.

#11
TV Spelling

Reading a television program guide is probably a part of many students' daily lives. In this activity, turn the table. Invite students to devise a schedule of television programs for the new fall season.

1. Provide a copy of the "TV Spelling" reproducible on page 18 for each student.

2. Explain to students that they will create titles for new television shows and then write brief descriptions of them.

3. Remind students to include spelling words in the title or description. Have them underline each spelling word.

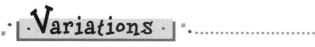

TV Spelling

Congratulations! You have just been hired by a local television station to schedule the TV programs for the new fall season. Your job is to come up with titles for the shows and to write brief descriptions of them. Use this week's spelling words in the titles or descriptions. Underline each spelling word, too.

Day   **Time**

_____   _____   Show Title: _____

                           Description: _____

                                          _____

                                          _____

                                          _____

_____   _____   Show Title: _____

                           Description: _____

                                          _____

                                          _____

                                          _____

_____   _____   Show Title: _____

                           Description: _____

                                          _____

                                          _____

                                          _____

_____   _____   Show Title: _____

                           Description: _____

                                          _____

                                          _____

                                          _____

Lost-and-Found Spelling

An announcement for an item that has been lost or found provides a wonderful spelling opportunity. Not only is it a real-world writing skill, but it can require the use of a variety of nouns, verbs, and adjectives. Give your students practice with this technical-writing technique as they incorporate their spelling words.

1. Bring in copies of the local paper. Divide the class into groups, and give each the classified section. Encourage the groups to locate the lost-and-found announcements in the classifieds. Have students take turns reading the listings within their groups.

2. As a class, discuss the information included in a lost-and-found ad. For example: the item lost, a description of the item, where it was lost, if a reward is being offered, whom to contact if found.

3. Have students write several lost-and-found ads incorporating their spelling words. Suggest that students review their spelling lists to come up with ideas.

4. Afterward, tell students to underline the spelling words in their ads.

> Lost
> A <u>tortoise</u>-shell kitten wearing an <u>orange collar</u>. Answers to the name of <u>Pancake</u>. Last seen in <u>garden</u> on <u>Imperial</u> Street. Call 555-0000

> Found
> An <u>official</u> and <u>important</u>-looking <u>briefcase</u> on the <u>cushion</u> of a couch in the lobby of hotel. Phone: 555-5555

Homophone Play

Recognizing homophones is an important spelling and vocabulary skill. To reinforce students' knowledge of homophones, invite them to write and draw zany pictures that illustrate both homophones.

1. Challenge students to identify words that are homophones in the spelling list. Or have students come up with homophones for the spelling words.

2. Invite students to create a picture that illustrates a pair of homophones.

3. Then tell students to write a caption for the drawing that not only explains it but that uses both homophones.

4. Have students underline the homophone pair.

> **Samples of Homophone Sentences**
> Barry is going to <u>bury</u> a <u>berry</u>.
> Sue was eating a <u>pair</u> of <u>pears</u>.
> A bird <u>flew</u> into a <u>flue</u>.

Magazine Maker

In this activity, students will use their spelling words to design magazine covers.
Generating ideas for magazine articles and titles will help them become familiar with the
words' meanings.

1. Start by showing students a variety of
   magazine covers. Invite volunteers to read
   the blurbs on the covers, pointing out that
   these tell a potential reader what the
   articles will be about inside the magazine.

2. Discuss how the cover helps to sell the
   magazine. How would students describe
   the writing style of the blurbs? What about
   the covers catches their eye?

3. Encourage students to create magazine
   covers of their own. Suggest that they
   first review their words for ideas. Explain
   that they can incorporate the words in
   a variety of ways. For example:
   - blurbs for the magazine cover
   - title for articles
   - the articles themselves
   - the names of people being inter-
     viewed or writing for the magazine
   - even the actual name of the magazine

4. Once students have written their ideas,
   let them design a magazine cover. Remind
   students that the magazine cover needs
   to attract the readers.

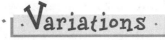

Variations

* Invite students to create covers for government-help pamphlets or pamphlets published
  by advertisers. Topic ideas include health, foot care, pet care, a healthy lawn, where to
  find a good deal on a car, purchasing a home, and so on.

* Have students apply their spelling words in a paragraph that describes the general
  theme or topic of a published magazine. Be sure they include the magazine's title in the
  paragraph. This will give them an opportunity to practice proper punctuation.

Newsy News Headlines

News headlines are another source for exciting spelling activities. Writing such headlines is an excellent way for students to practice not only spelling, but word meaning as well.

1. Bring in a few copies of the front pages of local or national newspapers. You could also make this a homework assignment, encouraging students to bring in newspapers from home.

2. Divide the class into groups and provide each group with front pages to discuss. Encourage students to read the headlines to each other, discussing their writing style and meaning. You can also have students predict what the article is about, and then have them read the first paragraph to confirm their predictions.

3. As a class, discuss the newspaper headlines in more detail. Speculate why newspaper headlines are written in short, catchy phrases. Guide students to ideas such as:
   - to attract the reader's attention
   - lack of room to write longer sentences
   - newspaper competition: Papers compete with each other, relaying the same information. Therefore, their headlines must be as exciting as possible, yet still stay focused on the main idea.

4. Brainstorm with students events that might make front-page news, and challenge students to suggest catchy headlines.

5. Now let students create "news" of their own. Ask them to write headlines and stories using words from their spelling lists.

6. Let students exchange their headlines with partners. Challenge the partners to identify and underline each spelling word.

Variations

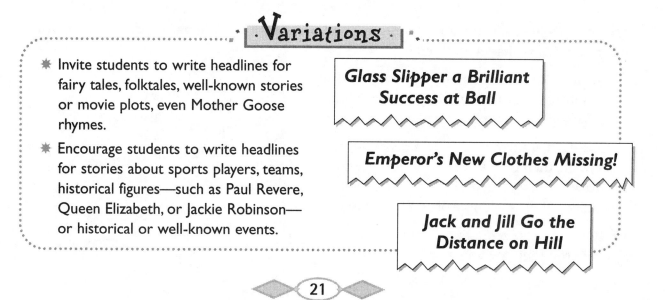

* Invite students to write headlines for fairy tales, folktales, well-known stories or movie plots, even Mother Goose rhymes.

* Encourage students to write headlines for stories about sports players, teams, historical figures—such as Paul Revere, Queen Elizabeth, or Jackie Robinson— or historical or well-known events.

Glass Slipper a Brilliant Success at Ball

Emperor's New Clothes Missing!

Jack and Jill Go the Distance on Hill

What's on the Menu?

For a "delectable" spelling activity, invite students to apply their spelling words as they create menus of pleasurable palate pleasers.

1 Review with students the ways restaurants use words, such as in the restaurant name, menu items, and food descriptions. If available, you could bring in take-out menus to pass around and inspire students.

2 Explain that you would like students to come up with their own menu ideas. Have them start by choosing a theme for their restaurants. What types of foods and dishes would they like to serve? What would their restaurants be called? Have students list ideas.

3 Then encourage them to design and write a menu. Provide students with the reproducibles on pages 23 and 24. Remind them to include spelling words in either the name of the dishor the description of the food.

4 Remind students to underline each spelling word.

Name _____ Date _____

Reproducible

What's on the Menu?

Create your own restaurant. Use your spelling words to write the menu. Come up with names for dishes, then describe them too. Fill in the menu card below.

Name of your restaurant: _Coyote Cafe_

SOUPS/SALADS

Name: _Orange and Tomato Rodeo Salad_ Price: _$3.95_
Description: _A tangy salad of fresh and juicy oranges and tomatoes served with a poppy seed dressing_

Name: _Stampede Potato Salad_ Price: _$3.50_
Description: _A heart healthy potato salad._

SANDWICHES

Name: _Around the Ranch Turkey Sandwich_ Price: _$5.95_
Description: _A tongue pleasing sandwich of turkey, cheese, and mustard._

Name: _Delicious Tuna Salad_ Price: _$5.50_
Description: _One of our most popular sandwiches. Choose from whole wheat or white bread._

Dear Diary

For this spelling activity, students can take on the identity of a literary character and write diary entries as that character.

1 Review with students the purpose of a diary or journal. Explain that diary entries express a person's thoughts, feelings, and/or secrets.

2 Ask each student to choose a character from a book, then direct them to write several diary entries for that character. Tell them to include their spelling words in the entries.

3 Have students reread their entries and underline the spelling words.

Dear Diary,
There is much excitement today! One of the king's <u>guards</u> delivered an invitation, inviting us to a grand ball. It is next <u>Thursday</u> in the <u>courtyard</u> of the palace. But I am very sad because my <u>horrible</u> stepmother will not let me attend. My stepsisters have been flaunting the invitation in my <u>direction</u> all day. I so wish I could go.

Name _____ Date _____

What's on the Menu?

Create your own restaurant. Use your spelling words to write the menu. Come up with names for dishes, then describe them too. Fill in the menu card below.

Name of your restaurant: _____

SOUPS/SALADS

Name: _____ Price: _____

Description: _____

_____

_____

Name: _____ Price: _____

Description: _____

_____

_____

SANDWICHES

Name: _____ Price: _____

Description: _____

_____

_____

Name: _____ Price: _____

Description: _____

_____

_____

What's on the Menu? (Continued)

DINNER SPECIALS

Name: _____   Price: _____

Description: _____

_____

_____

Name: _____   Price: _____

Description: _____

_____

_____

Name: _____   Price: _____

Description: _____

_____

_____

DESSERTS

Name: _____   Price: _____

Description: _____

_____

Name: _____   Price: _____

Description: _____

_____

Puzzle Pairs

Learning spelling words is more than knowing the correct letters and letter order. Spelling also means knowing word definitions and recognizing the meanings of words. Encourage students to solve spelling puzzles as they match words and definitions to put puzzle pieces together.

1. Reproduce the puzzle patterns on page 26. Provide students with as many copies as necessary so they have enough puzzle pairs for each spelling word.

2. Explain that for each puzzle pair, students will write a spelling word on one puzzle piece and its definition on the other.

3. Tell students to cut out and cut apart each puzzle piece.

4. Give each student a large envelope or folder in which to put the puzzle pieces.

5. Let students exchange puzzle envelopes with partners. Challenge the partners to match the words with their definitions.

6. Tell the partners to look over the matched puzzle pieces, making sure they are correct.

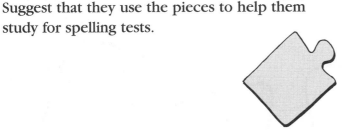

7. Let students take apart their own puzzle pieces, place them back in the envelope, then store them. Suggest that they use the pieces to help them study for spelling tests.

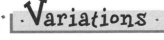

Variations

Suggest that students use the puzzle pieces to
* write antonyms or synonyms for each word;
* write a sentence in which the word makes sense, leaving a space for the missing word.

Puzzle Pairs Patterns

Yellow-Pages Spelling

Students may have a pretty good idea about some of the things they can find in the Yellow Pages phone directory, but they may be surprised at the incredible variety of products and services listed. With this activity, students will hone their Yellow Pages directory skills, while at the same time practicing their spelling words.

1 First, invite students to look at several pages from a Yellow-Pages phone book. Direct students to list the information they see. Have them take notes about how the information is arranged.

2 Tell students to pick a page to serve as a model.

3 Then have students work with partners to write ads and entries for a Yellow-Pages page that include their spelling words. Encourage them to write several types of ads, challenging them to include as many words as possible. Suggest that students be as creative as possible in writing, designing, and illustrating the ads.

4 When the ads are completed, have students underline their spelling words.

Tree Removal
Sugar's Tree Service
Serving St. Charles County for 25 years.
Tree removal of any size.
Insured for your protection.
555-1214

Motels
Martin's Motel
Single and double rooms
333 Council Avenue
For a simple night's rest
call 555-0101

Collage Magic

A collage is an artistic way for students to consider and comprehend the meanings of their spelling words. In order to construct their collages, students will need these materials: old magazines and newspapers; glue; card stock, approximately 9" x 12"; scissors.

1 Let students select magazines or newspapers from your collection. Instruct them to flip through the magazines to find pictures they feel represent the meanings of various spelling words. Have students cut out the pictures.

2 Ask students to glue their pictures onto the card stock in collage fashion, with some of the pictures overlapping.

3 Have students write each spelling word within or around the corresponding picture.

* Challenge students to find pictures that show the opposite meaning of each spelling word.

* Tell students not to label the pictures with the spelling words. Instead, challenge another student to match each picture with the correct spelling word.

* Divide the class into groups and assign different words from the spelling list to each group. Invite the groups to work on a class collage, cutting out as many pictures as they can to represent the spelling words.

#21
Rules Rule

What rules might your students choose if you gave them a chance to be in charge for a day? If they were in charge of their homes? Their town? How about their own made-up country? Give students that opportunity—in an imaginary way—as they practice their spelling words.

1 First, talk with students about the purpose of rules. Brainstorm rules students are familiar with, recalling rules for school, home, and so on.

2 Then direct each student to choose a situation in which she or he would like to be in charge. For example, "If I were in charge of our school, I would . . .," "If I were in charge of my own country, I would . . ."

3 Tell students to make a list of rules for the situation. Make sure they include their spelling words. The rules can be silly or serious.

4 Have students read over their rules and underline each spelling word.

Rules for Parents

1. Parents must make their <u>conversation</u> to a friend shorter.
2. You'll make an <u>invention</u> to do kid's homework.
3. You'll have an <u>occupation</u> of candy making so you can give kids the candy.
4. You'll give a <u>selection</u> of desserts every night to your child.
5. Always help your child with <u>multiplication</u> problems.
6. You'll make your house an <u>attraction</u> to kids.

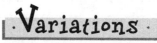

· **Variations** ·

* Have students choose a professional sports team. Ask them to write rules for the team that explain either appropriate player behavior or the game. Remind students that they are to include spelling words.

* Point out to students that in society, some rules are also laws. Review the purpose of laws, reminding students that laws should be followed and not broken. Talk with students about laws that their community might have. Ask students to write laws for their town using the spelling words. The laws can be real or ones they make up.

T-Time Lessons

An important aspect of spelling is recognizing words and their relationships to other words. For example, are words synonyms or antonyms of each other? How is a word used in a sentence? In addition, students can consider what they think a word means, then discover for themselves if their ideas are correct. In this activity students will be given a chance to see words in a new way and build their vocabularies.

1. Provide each student with a copy of the reproducible on page 30.

2. Discuss with students what you mean by an "example." Share the sample on this page.

3. In comparison, talk about what an *incorrect* example would be.

4. Challenge students to complete the **T** using their spelling words. Have students write what they think the word means, provide an example, then look the word up and provide an incorrect example.

Word	
What I think the word means	Dictionary definition
Example	Incorrect example

victory	
To win at something	A win in a battle or contest
The cornhuskers win the game.	The game ended in a tie.

Variations

* Challenge students to come up with antonyms and synonyms for each word, rather than definitions. Provide each student with a copy of page 31.

* Encourage students to examine words with prefixes and suffixes. Tell students to write the word with the prefix or suffix in the top part of the **T**. Below that, have them write an example that shows the word's meaning. Provide each student with a copy of page 32.

Spelling Word	
Synonym	Antonym
Example	Example

Root Word	
Prefix or Suffix	Prefix or Suffix
Example	Example

T-Time Definitions

Fill in each **T** with your ideas about the word. First, write the spelling word on the line. Then fill in the **T**, following the example at the right.

Spelling Word

1. _____ *giddy* _____

What I think the word means	Dictionary Definition
silly	dizzy; frivolous
Example	**Incorrect Example**
Alex was giddy with excitement about the party.	The solemn tone of the play left her giddy.

Spelling Word

1. _____

What I think the word means	Dictionary Definition
Example	**Incorrect Example**

Spelling Word

2. _____

What I think the word means	Dictionary Definition
Example	**Incorrect Example**

Spelling Word

3. _____

What I think the word means	Dictionary Definition
Example	**Incorrect Example**

Spelling Word

4. _____

What I think the word means	Dictionary Definition
Example	**Incorrect Example**

Spelling Word

5. _____

What I think the word means	Dictionary Definition
Example	**Incorrect Example**

Spelling Word

6. _____

What I think the word means	Dictionary Definition
Example	**Incorrect Example**

Name _____ Date _____

T–Time Antonyms and Synonyms

Fill in each **T** with your ideas about the word. First, write the spelling word on the line. Then fill in the **T**, following the example on the right.

Spelling Word

1. _____ Victory _____

Synonym	Antonym
win	loss
Example	Example
The game was a win.	The game was a loss.

Spelling Word

1. _____

Synonym	Antonym
Example	Example

Spelling Word

2. _____

Synonym	Antonym
Example	Example

Spelling Word

3. _____

Synonym	Antonym
Example	Example

Spelling Word

4. _____

Synonym	Antonym
Example	Example

Spelling Word

5. _____

Synonym	Antonym
Example	Example

Spelling Word

6. _____

Synonym	Antonym
Example	Example

T-Time Prefixes and Suffixes

Fill in each **T** with your ideas about the word. First, write the spelling word on the line. Then fill in the **T**, following the example on the right.

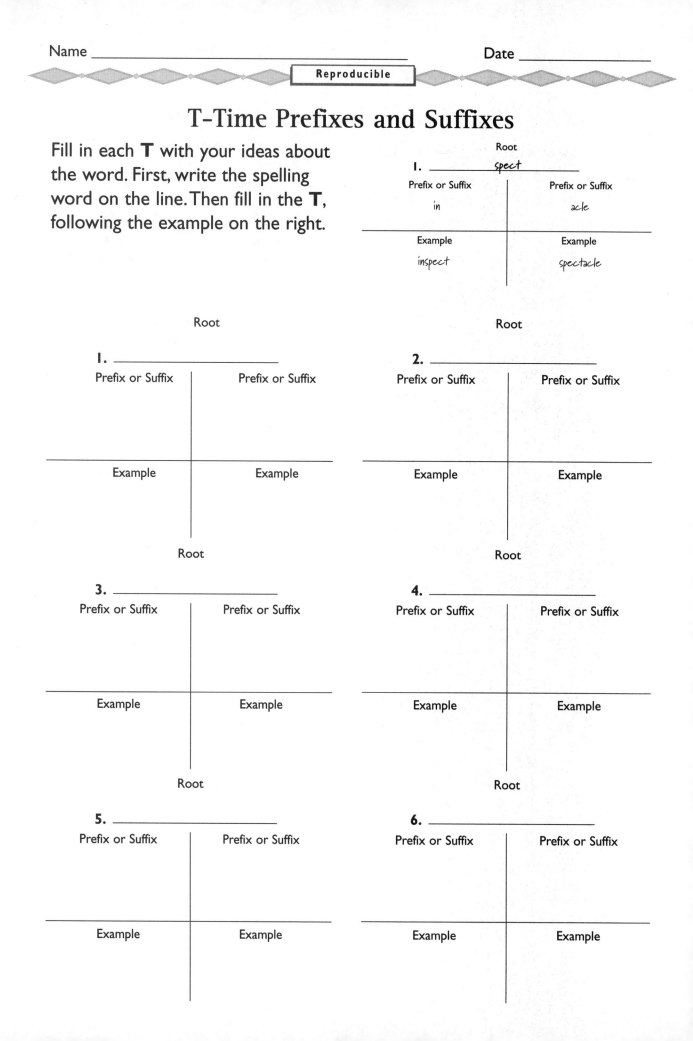

Root

1. _____ spect _____

Prefix or Suffix	Prefix or Suffix
in	acle
Example	Example
inspect	spectacle

Root

1. _____

Prefix or Suffix	Prefix or Suffix
Example	Example

Root

2. _____

Prefix or Suffix	Prefix or Suffix
Example	Example

Root

3. _____

Prefix or Suffix	Prefix or Suffix
Example	Example

Root

4. _____

Prefix or Suffix	Prefix or Suffix
Example	Example

Root

5. _____

Prefix or Suffix	Prefix or Suffix
Example	Example

Root

6. _____

Prefix or Suffix	Prefix or Suffix
Example	Example

Marvelous Machines

Let your students' imaginations run wild! Invite them to not only "invent" unusual machines, but to apply their spelling words as they name and advertise their creations.

1. Ahead of time, collect catalogs or advertising fliers for machines or appliances. Bring the materials to class.

2. Invite students to work in small groups to look through the material. Encourage them to notice the various advertising styles and the types of machines they see. Have students consider questions such as: What about the ads is appealing? How do the ads describe the machines? Do students feel compelled to buy the products? Why or why not?

3. Brainstorm with the class machines that it might be fun to have, such as a machine that completes or checks homework, a machine that warns when a brother or sister enters the bedroom, or a machine that could make a bed.

4. Then give each student a 9-by-18-inch piece of paper. Encourage students to design and draw their new-machine ideas. Tell them to leave room on their paper for writing.

5. When their drawings are complete, challenge students to write an ad for the machine on the same sheet of paper. Explain that ads should be colorful and should show special features of the product. Remind students that they need to include their spelling words in their ads. Spelling words can also label parts of the machine or be part of its name.

6. Ask students to underline each spelling word.

Graveyard Spelling

Epitaphs on tombstones might seem like a "grave" writing assignment, but the uniqueness of the idea is sure to liven up an everyday spelling activity.

1 Start by brainstorming with students ideas about things others might say about a heroic or famous person who has died. The person can be someone well known in history or the entertainment industry, or even a book character. List students' ideas on chart paper. Leave the list posted where students can refer to it.

2 Then explain that the words written on a tombstone are called epitaphs. Speculate about why people would want to write about others on their tombstones. For example:
- ♦ to honor the person's memory
- ♦ to inform others about the life of that person
- ♦ to remember the person's accomplishments

3 Provide each student with a copy of the graveyard reproducible on page 35. Tell students that you would like them to write epitaphs about people. The epitaphs should be silly and entertaining. They can even rhyme. The only requirement is that they need to include their spelling words. You might share with students the examples at right.

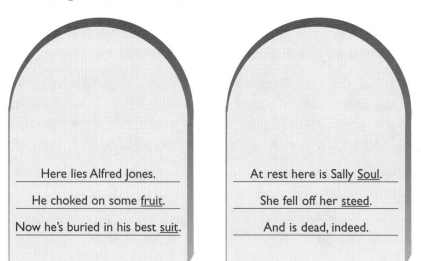

Here lies Alfred Jones.

He choked on some <u>fruit</u>.

Now he's buried in his best <u>suit</u>.

At rest here is Sally <u>Soul</u>.

She fell off her <u>steed</u>.

And is dead, indeed.

4 Have students underline the spelling words they used in the epitaphs.

Variations

- ✳ Challenge students to write epitaphs, either serious or silly, for famous people from history.
- ✳ Encourage students to write epitaphs for fairy-tale characters or other well-known story characters.
- ✳ Challenge students to write entertaining epitaphs that have a special twist on a well-known fable, such as a spider who was bitten by a poisonous boy or a snake that was swallowed by a frog.

Reproducible

Graveyard Spelling

Write an epitaph in each tombstone below. Underline your spelling words.

Analogy Spelling

Analogies help students consider things in diverse ways. They require not only a comprehension of word meanings, but knowledge of a word's relationship to another word. Analogies are ideal for spelling practice.

1. Before starting, challenge students to figure out the relationships in these analogies:
   - Lieutenant is to crew as manager is to employee.
   - Scholar is to learner as instructor is to teacher.
   - Handle is to shovel as knob is to door.

2. Brainstorm relationships that could be described in an analogy. For example:
   - part to whole
   - similar words
   - how something is done
   - how items are used
   - opposite words

3. With the class, compose several analogies.

4. Then challenge students to write analogies on their own, using their spelling words. Have them underline each spelling word.

#26

Billboard City

Billboards are found along many streets and highways. In this lesson, students will create interesting billboards for travelers to read.

1. Start by letting students tell about billboards they have seen. Discuss the purpose of the billboards.

2. Tell students they'll be creating their own mini-billboards. Have students review their spelling words for ideas to use in creating their billboards.

3. Encourage students to color and illustrate their billboards. Have them underline each spelling word.

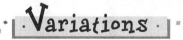

Variations

* Encourage students to use their spelling words to create small billboards that might be useful around school. For example, billboards could advertise the quality of lunches, or products at the school store, or recreation opportunities on the school athletic field.

* Invite students to incorporate their spelling words into billboards that advertise a local restaurant, grocery store, gas station, library, or other community service.

How-to Pamphlets

Invite your students to show their expertise! Have them create how-to pamphlets with their spelling words that explain how to complete a particular task.

1. Brainstorm ideas for topics on which students are experts, such as baby-sitting, taking care of a dog, washing a car, mastering a video game, and so on.

2. Choose one task, and model for students how to think about the steps someone would need to follow to be successful at this job.

3. Now ask each student to choose a task at which he or she is an expert. Tell students to write down step-by-step instructions that describe how to complete the task. Remind students that they must include spelling words in their how-to explanations.

4. Have students underline their spellings words.

5. Encourage students to include illustrations and diagrams to bring their how-to pamphlets to life.

How to Wash a Car

1. First, <u>shower</u> the car with a light mist of water from a hose.
2. Next, use a <u>moist</u> sponge and soapy water to scrub one section of the car in a <u>circular</u> motion.
3. Then rinse off the soap, but don't "<u>drown</u>" the car!
4. Continue working your way <u>around</u> the car, section by section, repeating steps 2 ad 3.
5. When done, rinse off the entire car one last time. As the car shines, dirt-free, you will feel <u>proud</u> of a job well done.

Movie Madness

Writing movie reviews encourages students to recall details, recount plot sequences, and share their own opinions. Incorporating their spelling words in their reviews will help students become more familiar with them. The reviews can be based on movies currently in the theater, or movies students have seen on television or video.

1. Obtain movie reviews from your local paper. Invite volunteers to read them aloud. Point out the tone and writing style, as well as the information they contain.

2. Start a list of phrases that movie critics might include in a review. The phrases can be mined from the actual movie reviews or from ideas generated during a brainstorming session. If any spelling words are used, underline them.

3 Then encourage each student to choose a movie to review. It can be a movie they enjoyed or a movie that disappointed them. As students write their reviews, encourage them to include as many spelling words as possible. Tell students to underline the words, too.

4 Invite students to share their critiques with the other "movie critics" in class.

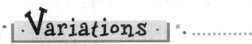

· Variations ·

* Let students write critiques of the various meals served in the cafeteria.

* Ask students to review books they are reading or have read.

* Have students write a review about a recent sporting event.

* Let students critique different school subjects.

#29
"Reasons Why" Spelling

How many different excuses have *you* heard about missing homework? Students are very adept at creating reasons why something did or did not happen. Build on this creativity by allowing students to channel their creative "excuses" in a spelling activity.

1 Write the situations below on the chalkboard. Invite students to read them.
- The groundhog did not see his shadow.
- A star fell from the sky.
- My dad/mom was late for work.
- A zebra lost its stripes.

2 Provide each student with the reproducible on page 39. Have students consider and write reasons why the situations above occurred. Let them come up with their own creative situations, too. Remind students that they need to include their spelling words in their writing. Tell them to underline the spelling words.

Situation: The football player didn't show up for his game.
Reasons why: 1. He promised his wife he would wash the <u>windows</u>.
2. He couldn't <u>afford</u> a taxi to the stadium.

Situation: The sun decided not to rise one morning.
Reasons why: 1. It was up too late watching the <u>circus</u> perform.
2. It got injured playing <u>tennis</u> and stayed in bed.

Reasons Why

Write about a strange situation. Then write two explanations, or "reasons why," that tell about it. Include as many spelling words as you can. Underline your spelling words, too.

Situation: _____

Reasons why: 1. _____

2. _____

Situation: _____

Reasons why: 1. _____

2. _____

Situation: _____

Reasons why: 1. _____

2. _____

Situation: _____

Reasons why: 1. _____

2. _____

Situation: _____

Reasons why: 1. _____

2. _____

Situation: _____

Reasons why: 1. _____

2. _____

Commercial Appeal

All commercials require the same thing—the use of words. During this activity students will become advertisers as they create their own commercials that include their spelling words. Encourage students to be as creative as they like, inventing both the products as well as the commercials.

1. Discuss with students commercials they have enjoyed, either in print form (such as in a magazine) or on television. Brainstorm with the class characteristics that not only make commercials appealing, but entice consumers to consider buying a product.

2. Encourage students to come up with ideas for commercials of their own. Have them start by reviewing their spelling lists to gather ideas. Explain that their commercials can be about a real product or a product they make up. Tell students to jot down ideas.

3. Then challenge students to write a script for the commercial characters or a product spokesperson.

4. Invite students to read their commercials to the class.

* Invite students to create commercials for the school store, an upcoming sporting event, a school dance, or any other prominent school activity or service.

* Suggest that students make commercials for the community, such as local businesses, public officials, recreation areas, and so on.

#31

Definition Selection

The way a word is used in a sentence often helps readers discover and reinforce the word's meaning. In this activity, students will write sentences that include the proper use of spelling words and then ask individuals to determine what the word means.

1. Reproduce copies of the activity sheet on page 42. Make sure each student has enough copies so he or she can write a sentence for each spelling word. Ask students to first write the spelling word, then to compose a sentence in which the word is used correctly. Next, have them write three possible definitions for each word. Only one definition should be correct.

2. Have students show their sentences and definitions to ten people who do not have that word list. The ten people can include teachers, students in other classes, or family members. Tell them to ask those ten people which definition is the correct one. Have them explain that the sentence should provide clues. Instruct students to record the answers.

3. Finally, encourage students to record their data on a graph that shows how many people knew the meanings of their spelling words.

* Have all the students compile their data into a class graph.

* Work with students to find the average number of people who knew the correct definitions.

* Ask students to write sentences in which the words are used *incorrectly*. Have them ask others if the words are correctly used, and graph the responses.

#32
Advice Is Nice

Invite your students to offer advice, while at the same time using their spelling words.

1. Bring in samples of advice columns from a local or national newspaper. Invite students to read the letters and responses aloud in class. Discuss the topics featured in the letters, then brainstorm other troublesome situations about which someone might write to an advice columnist about. The situations can be comical as well as moderately serious.

2. Have students draft their own letters to an advice columnist in which they use their spelling words.

3. Afterward, have students answer their own letters, suggesting advice, and again incorporating spelling words. Make sure students underline each spelling word.

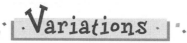

* Let students exchange letters and suggest their own advice. Encourage students to share their advice letters, comparing their thoughts on the same situation.

* Ask students to consider writing a letter from a historical figure. The matter could be about something that happened in history or something they make up. They should then write a letter back, offering advice.

Advice to George Washington: Benedict Arnold seems to be a <u>liar</u>. He might not be there in your <u>hour</u> of need.

Definition Selection

Write your spelling word on the first line. Then write a sentence in which the word is used correctly. Finally, write three definitions for the word: one definition is correct, the other two are incorrect. Ask family and friends to figure out the correct definition.

Spelling Word: _____

Sentence: _____

_____

Definition 1: _____

Definition 2: _____

Definition 3: _____

Spelling Word: _____

Sentence: _____

_____

Definition 1: _____

Definition 2: _____

Definition 3: _____

Spelling Word: _____

Sentence: _____

_____

Definition 1: _____

Definition 2: _____

Definition 3: _____

Good News and Bad News

Countering bad news with a dose of good news is a common tactic in adult interaction. On the student level, it provides a chance to think creatively while considering spelling words. It's also a great way to reinforce an understanding of root words.

1. Begin by telling students that you have some good news and some bad news: "The bad news is that it's time for spelling. The good news is that the exercise is fun and you can be as creative as you wish!"

2. Discuss with students the concept of sharing "good news" and "bad news" at the same time. Point out to students that adults often do this so the bad news does not seem quite so bad in light of the good news. Brainstorm ideas for some good news/bad news situations. Try to keep the situations light, even comical.

3. Challenge students to write their own good news/bad news sentences, using their spelling words. Tell them to underline each spelling word.

The bad news is there was an <u>accident</u> in the cafeteria. The good news is there are no <u>mushrooms</u> for lunch.

4. When finished, invite students to share their sentences with the class.

School Dazed

Reading, writing, 'rithmetic. These are the subjects students are most familiar with. But if kids could choose school subjects, what would they *really* like to learn about? Find out by inviting students to come up with classes that they would like to take in school, while including their spelling words in their ideas.

Senior <u>Ambulance</u> Driving
<u>Unforgettable</u> Lunchroom <u>Etiquette</u>
<u>Advanced</u> <u>Underwater</u> Home Economics
Teacher-<u>Disappearing</u> Science

1. Pose the idea of new school subjects to your class. Motivate your students with the subject topics and titles at right.

2. Challenge students to come up with their own silly subject ideas. Have them write interesting and clever classroom titles using their spelling words.

3. Invite students to share their ideas with the class. Speculate with students about what the silly classes might be about.

4. As a follow-up and to reinforce spelling words, let students write course descriptions for each school-dazed subject.

#35

What If? Spelling

To encourage higher-order thinking, we as educators often ask students to hypothesize what might have happened or what could happen if certain variables are changed in a situation. For example: What could happen if life is discovered on another planet? What might have happened if Cinderella had not lost her glass slipper? Such intriguing possibilities lend themselves well to critical- and creative-thinking spelling exercises.

1) Introduce the activity by suggesting some what-if? possibilities, such as those in the box shown here. Encourage students to think about how the world, society, or a story might be different.

2) Challenge students to think about and write their own what-if? sentences, using their spelling words. Ask them to underline the spelling words, too.

3) If time allows, encourage students to build upon their ideas, writing short stories or paragraphs based on their what-if? possibilities.

> • What if Columbus had gone on a <u>vacation</u> instead of an <u>expedition</u>?
> • What if Florida wanted to be part of another <u>nation</u>?
> • What if you didn't have to pay for <u>admission</u> to a movie theater?
> • What if Goldilocks had asked <u>permission</u> before she entered the home of the three bears?

Variations

* Have students exchange their what-if? sentences with classmates. Encourage students to write their own ideas about what might or could happen.

* Suggest that students pose their what-if? questions to an adult. Have them share the responses in class.

* Instruct students to write what-if? questions directed to famous people from history, entertainment, or sports. For example: "Michael Jordan—what if you had never played for the Chicago Bulls?"

#36

Wish on a Star Spelling

The notion of making a wish and it coming true is magical. Students make wishes when they blow out birthday candles. They imagine what they would ask for if granted three wishes, or they gaze up at the night sky and wish on a star. Turn the magic of wishing into a spelling activity.

1) Provide each student with one copy of the pattern on page 46.

2. Encourage students to review their spelling words and to consider wishes that could incorporate the words. Explain that the wishes may be funny or serious.

3. Ask students to write their wishes along the outer edges of the star, underlining the spelling words. They can write within the star or on the back of the page if they need extra room. (Explain that wishing the spelling words would go away is not an option!)

4. Let students take their "wish on a star" spelling pages home, or decorate the classroom with star wishes.

Variations

* Encourage students to make wishes for friends or family members.
* Suggest that they make wishes for political figures or for changes in the community.
* Have them choose a famous person and write wishes that the person might write.

#37
Words of Wisdom

Words of wisdom can come in many forms. They can be idioms, clichés, or proverbs. They can be learned from families, reading, role models, or experience. In this activity, students will compose their own words of wisdom that rely on their spelling words. Homophones and words with common roots, such as *wide* and *width*, work well for this activity.

1. Brainstorm with students proverbs, clichés, or idioms they know, such as: *Don't cry over spilt milk. Better safe than sorry. I'm tickled pink. A penny saved is a penny earned. Never look back. Keep your chin up.* Discuss with students where they have heard these "words of wisdom." Also talk about the purpose of such sayings—for example, easy ways to remember something, small lessons one learns through experience, and so on.

> Don't <u>laugh</u> at others or the <u>laughter</u> may be on you.
> You can't always go <u>straight</u> through a <u>strait</u>.
> How <u>wide</u> the smile shows the <u>width</u> of the heart.

2. Have students use their spelling words to compose their own words of wisdom. To broaden the exercise, explain that the sayings need not be serious, but can be silly, too. Tell students to underline their spelling words in each proverb.

3. Let students share their words of wisdom with the class. Ask the rest of the class to explain what the saying means and to identify the spellings words.

Wish on a Star Pattern

Wanted Posters

Although in real life "Wanted" posters are very serious matters, in cartoons, movies, and stories, Wanted posters are fun illustrations that mix words and pictures to describe a felon on the loose. For this activity, students will pose as sketch artists for the FBI, designing posters for imaginary criminals. Along with an illustration, students will include descriptions that incorporate their spelling words.

1. Discuss with the class the idea of Wanted posters. Let students share any they may have seen on television, in movies, or in books. Discuss the information presented on these posters, and list their ideas on the chalkboard.

2. Suggest to students that they are sketch artists, working for the FBI. Their job is to draw a picture of a wanted felon and provide information to aid in the felon's capture. Encourage students to come up with silly or serious offenses and descriptions that include the words on their spelling lists.

3. Pass out drawing paper, and invite students to design their Wanted posters. Suggest that first they draw the wanted felon.

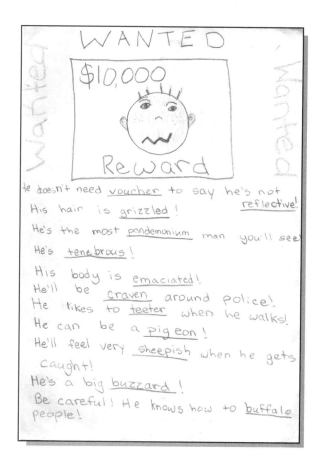

4. Instruct students to then describe the felon, including any distinguishing physical features, characteristics, hobbies, or habits. Tell them to include the reason the felon is wanted, where the person might be found, where the person was last seen, and any other information they feel would help the FBI.

5. Have the students underline the spelling words.

6. Display the Wanted posters around the room.

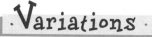

Variations

* Have students make Wanted posters for notorious villains in history.
* Let students make wanted posters for fairy-tale villains.

Finger Words

To many students, sign language is like a secret code. It allows students to communicate secretly with one another, and it also builds an appreciation and understanding for those who are hearing impaired. Encourage students to practice their sign-language skills as they employ the signs to spell words.

1. Provide each student with a copy of the sign-language alphabet below.

2. Have students work in pairs. Ask one student to spell a word in sign language. Challenge the other partner to write down the word.

3. Let students confer, confirming ideas and accurate spelling.

4. Tell students to take turns signing their spelling words.

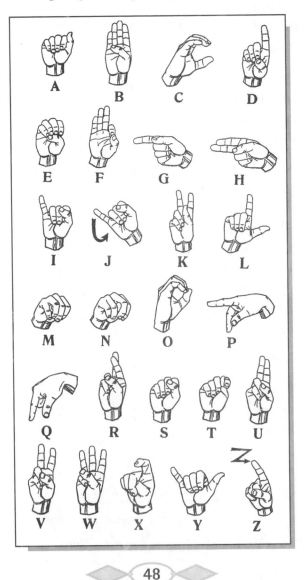

Spelling Maps

Along with lines and symbols, maps are full of words. Creating a spelling map encourages students to practice spelling their words as they come up with names for streets, buildings, parks, and other places.

1 Begin by reviewing with students the features of a map. You might pull down your wall map or present a local street map as a guide. Point out to students the place names featured on the map.

2 Then invite each student to design a map for an imaginary city. Along with the various city streets, suggest that their maps include some of the following locations:

Map Features		
bus stop	church	grocery store
library	post office	temple
fire station	police station	city hall
shopping mall	school	bridge
park	airport	hospital
gas station	lake	fast-food restaurant
map scale	city name	compass rose

3 After drawing their maps, have students use their spelling words to name and label each place.

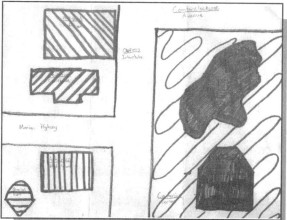

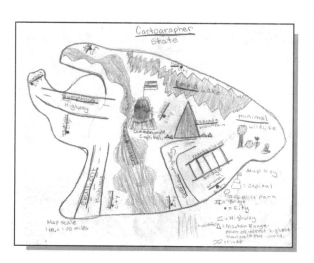

✳ Invite students to expand their imaginary cities by creating maps for imaginary states or countries. These maps might include:

Expanded Map Features

mountain range	lake	cities	river	plain	towns	volcano
state capital	bay	sea	basin	ocean	peninsula	waterfall
historical landmark	delta	dam	highway	map key	map scale	compass rose

#41
Alien Translations

The science-fiction genre is a creative and fascinating world to explore. Whether in television series, movies, or books, the idea of creatures from other worlds entertains audiences, both young and old. Invite students to create their own outer-space beings as they practice their spelling words.

1. Start by reviewing the science-fiction genre. Let students share their favorite movies, characters, or books that have a science-fiction twist.

2. Then invite students to draw their own creatures from outer space. Encourage students to be as creative as possible with their aliens, suggesting extra arms, unusual body parts, antennae, silly colors or patterns, and so on. Tell students to let their imaginations run wild.

3. Also ask students to illustrate the alien's habitat, such as a yard, the spaceship, special physical features of its planet, and so on.

4. To apply their spelling words, have students identify and label parts of the alien's body or environment. For example, an arm might be called a *strait*.

5. Explain that once the alien is labeled, those of us on Earth will need a dictionary to translate the terms. On the back of the picture, ask students to write the spelling words and their "English translations," or definitions.

6. Invite students to share their outer-space aliens with the class.

Variations ·

✳ During Halloween, let students create imaginary monsters, labeling the monsters' body parts and environments.

✳ Have students label the body parts with synonyms or antonyms of the spelling words, then translate with the actual spelling words.

Butterfly Mobiles

These stunning works of art will brighten up any classroom—and spelling exercise! As students put together the mobiles, they'll be putting their spelling and vocabulary skills to work.

1 Copy the butterfly reproducible page for each student. Have students trace around and cut out the butterfly pattern to make more butterflies.

2 On writing paper, direct students to write a sentence for each of their spelling words. Make sure they underline the spelling words.

3 Tell students to rewrite the sentences on the butterfly wings, one sentence per wing, front and back. (In other words, each butterfly cutout should have four sentences.)

4 Let students color the outside edge of the butterfly wings with bright colors and patterns.

How to Assemble the Mobile

1. Direct students to cut out the round mobile hanger and all their butterflies.

2. For sturdier bases, have students glue the base to construction paper before cutting it out.

3. Give each student three pieces of yarn, each about 20 inches long.

4. Demonstrate how to poke small holes through the dots on the mobile hanger with a pencil.

5. Instruct students to insert one end of the thread through dot A. Have them stretch the other end across the top of the mobile to dot B, then thread through dot B. For balance, the threads dangling from the mobile should be the same length.

6. Have them repeat the procedure with the second strand, threading it through dots C and D.

7. Tell students to tape one butterfly to the end of each dangling thread.

8. Ask students to thread the third piece of yarn through dot E, then tape the thread to the hanger.

9. Hang the mobiles from the middle thread. Invite students to read each other's butterfly sentences to appreciate the many ways in which the spelling words were used.

Variations

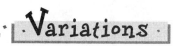

* Let students write the word on one wing and its definition on the other wing or on the back of the same wing.

* Adapt this activity for different seasons or holidays by using one of the patterns on page 53.

Mobile Base and Butterfly Pattern

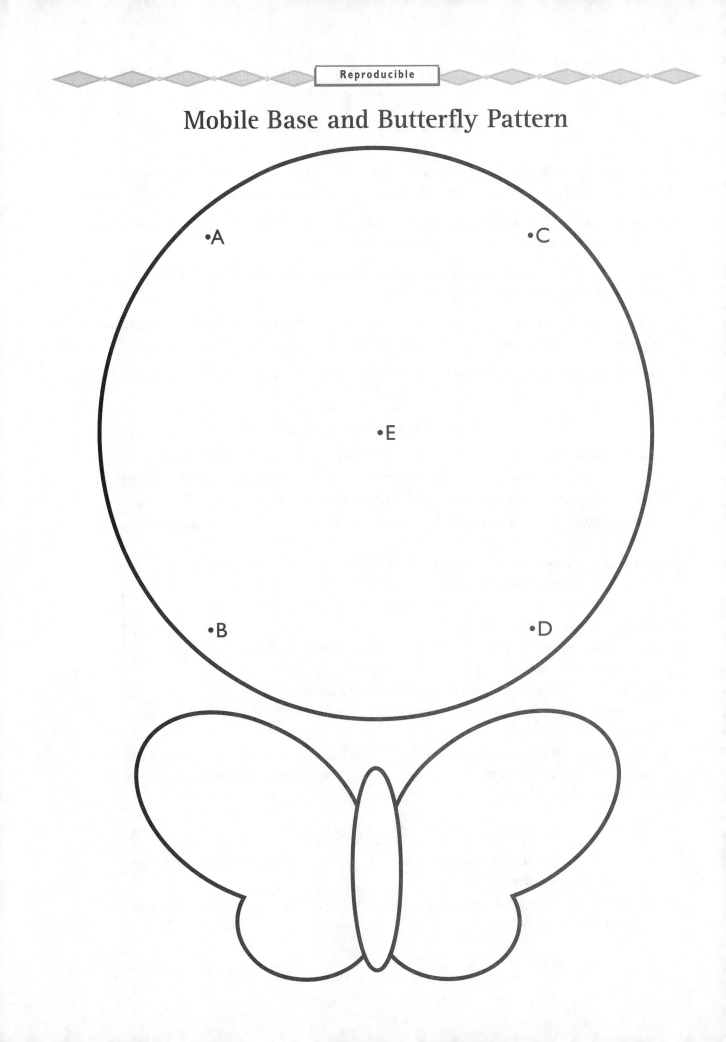

Alternate Mobile Patterns

Sssilly Sssnakes

This spelling activity will capture the interest of your kinesthetic learners. As students write their spelling words on these silly snakes, they will reinforce how each word is spelled and how they relate to other words, either alphabetically or grammatically.

1. Draw an outline of a snake's curving body on the chalkboard, making it wide enough for words to fit inside. Pass out drawing paper, and invite students to draw their own snakes.

2. Have students divide the snake into sections, one for each spelling word.

3. Then direct students to write the first word that appears alphabetically on their spelling lists on the head of their snakes.

4. Tell students to write one spelling word on each remaining section, *not* in alphabetical order.

5. Instruct students to then cut apart the snake sections.

6. Now have students arrange the body parts in alphabetical order and glue the entire snake onto a sheet of paper.

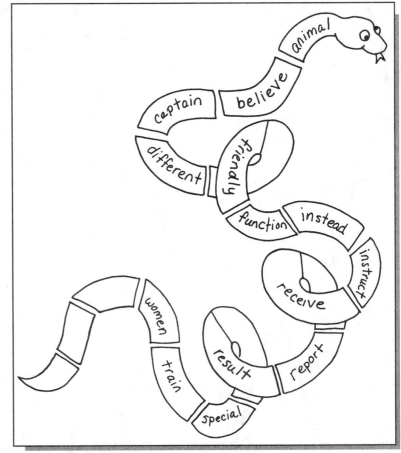

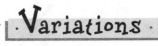

* Instead of arranging the snake's body alphabetically, have students arrange the words according to parts of speech.

* Have students come up with their own ideas for arranging the words.

Board-Game Spelling

Most students will agree—learning is more fun when games are involved. This spelling activity invites students to create their own ideas for a board game that incorporates their spelling words.

1. Talk with students about popular board games they enjoy. You might have one on hand as an example. Point out the words and phrases within the game-board squares, as well as the words, phrases, and sentences on playing cards. Explain that you would like students to develop their own board game.

2. Have students work in small groups. Provide each group with two copies of the game board and one copy of the cards from pages 56 and 57. Tell students to turn one game board upside down, and then to match the halves of the game board and tape the game board together.

3. Direct students to contemplate possible game ideas, referring to games they know.

4. Tell students to begin by writing down the rules of their game. Explain that the game instructions can include spelling words, if appropriate.

5. When the rules have been established, encourage students to fill in the playing cards and game-board spaces. This could be a simple matter of writing a spelling word within a square or playing card, or incorporating the words into more lengthy phrases or sentences.

6. When ready, suggest that the group try out the game, fixing any problems with the instructions, the game board, or the playing cards.

7. During another class session, invite the groups to exchange game boards and enjoy their classmates' spelling games.

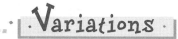

Variations

If time is short, let students play the following game with partners.

* Ahead of time, write one spelling word on each playing card. Cut the cards apart. Create the game board, and designate "Start" and "Finish" points. Place the playing cards facedown in the center of the game board. Set up dice and a marker for each player.

* Tell Player A to choose the first card and read it to Player B. Player B must spell the word correctly.

* If Player B does spell the word correctly, the player rolls the dice and moves along the board that number of spaces. If Player B does not spell the word correctly, it is the next player's turn.

* After each chance, successful or unsuccessful, the players switch roles.

* Play continues until the first player reaches the end of the game board.

Spelling Game Board

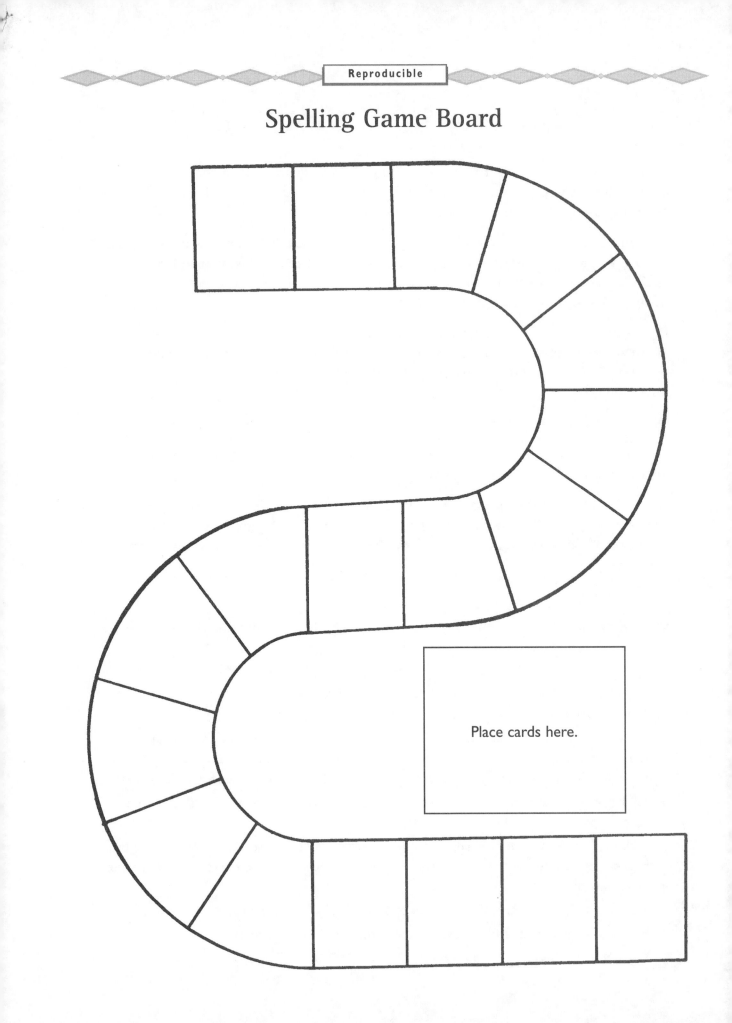

Place cards here.

Playing Cards

◆ Spell Well! ◆	◆ Spell Well! ◆	◆ Spell Well! ◆	◆ Spell Well! ◆
◆ Spell Well! ◆	◆ Spell Well! ◆	◆ Spell Well! ◆	◆ Spell Well! ◆
◆ Spell Well! ◆	◆ Spell Well! ◆	◆ Spell Well! ◆	◆ Spell Well! ◆
◆ Spell Well! ◆	◆ Spell Well! ◆	◆ Spell Well! ◆	◆ Spell Well! ◆

Spelling Concentration

During the traditional game of "Concentration," players must overturn cards to find matching pairs. "Spelling Concentration" encourages students to test their vocabulary skills as they match spelling words with the words' definitions.

1. Select 16 words for review. Make two copies of the reproducible cards on page 57. Write each word on one set of the 16 cards and then write the definition of each word on the other set.

2. Shuffle the cards and place them facedown on a table. Invite two students to the table to play "Spelling Concentration."

3. Explain that each player takes turns flipping over two cards to find a spelling word, then the matching definition. If the cards don't match, players turn them facedown again. If the cards do match, players take the pair. Players who make a match may go again.

4. At the end of the game, the player with the greatest number of pairs wins.

Variations

* Players can also try to match words that are synonyms, antonyms, or homonyms.

#46

Picture-Perfect Word Drawing

As another practice drill, invite students to draw pictures that encompass all their spelling words. The pictures should be creative and fun and demonstrate students' understanding of word meanings.

1. Provide each student with a large sheet of drawing paper and colored pencils, markers, or crayons.

2. Tell students that you would like them to create a picture that includes and illustrates each word. The drawing should be a single scene.

3. Suggest that students first review their spelling words, looking for inspiration. Upon completing their drawings, have students label each part with the correct spelling word.

4. Let students compare their drawings with those of others in the class who have the same spelling lists. Students might be surprised to see the different ideas of their classmates.

Spelling Contracts

Spelling contracts are excellent for independent work. Each student is asked to choose which activity he or she will complete in a specific time period or for a specific grade. Because the student chooses the activity, he or she feels in control of the learning process, and therefore is motivated to do a better job. Here are two suggestions for ways to use the contracts:

1. Post a list of the various spelling activities. Ask students to fill in the spaces on their contracts with the activities they want to complete.

2. Fill in the spaces with the activities before the contracts are reproduced. Invite students to choose which activities they want to complete.

#47
Calendar Contract

Use the contract on page 61 when you want students to complete a specific number of activities for a week or a month.

#48
Pizza Contract

The Pizza Contract on page 62 encourages students to complete a specific number of activities in order to earn a specific grade.

Spelling Squares Contract

Students use this contract to choose activities that will form a winning tic-tac-toe row, either vertically, horizontally, or diagonally. Provide each student with a copy of the "Spelling Squares Contract" on page 63. As students complete their spelling activities, have them check off each activity on the tic-tac-toe contract. Encourage them to complete enough activities to make a winning tic-tac-toe combination.

Bingo Contract

With this contract, students choose activities that will form a winning bingo row, either vertically, horizontally, or diagonally. (You may want to add more free spaces to the contract.) Provide each student with a copy of the "Bingo Contract" on page 64. As students complete their spelling activities, have them check off each activity on the bingo contract. Encourage them to complete enough activities to make a winning bingo combination.

Spelling Contracts

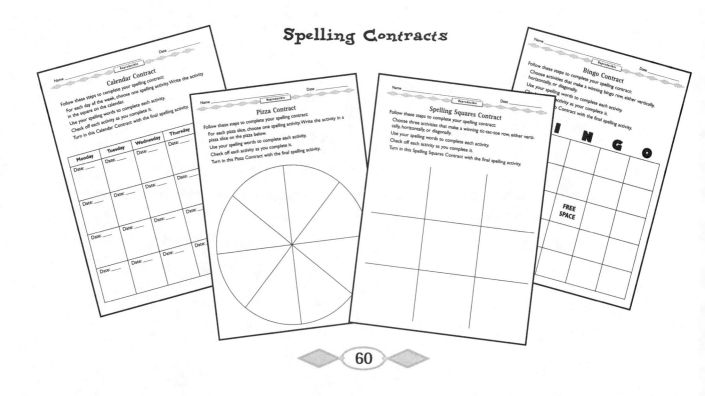

Name _____   Date _____

Calendar Contract

Follow these steps to complete your spelling contract:

1. For each day of the week, choose one spelling activity. Write the activity title in the square on the calendar.

2. Use your spelling words to complete each activity.

3. Check off each activity as you complete it. Write the date, too.

4. Turn in this Calendar Contract with the final spelling activity.

Monday	**Tuesday**	**Wednesday**	**Thursday**	**Friday**
Date: _____	Date: _____	Date: _____	Date: _____	Date: _____
Date: _____	Date: _____	Date: _____	Date: _____	Date: _____
Date: _____	Date: _____	Date: _____	Date: _____	Date: _____
Date: _____	Date: _____	Date: _____	Date: _____	Date: _____

Pizza Contract

Follow these steps to complete your spelling contract:

1. For each pizza slice, choose one spelling activity. Write the activity title on the slice.

2. Use your spelling words to complete each activity.

3. Check off each activity as you complete it.

4. Turn in this Pizza Contract with the final spelling activity.

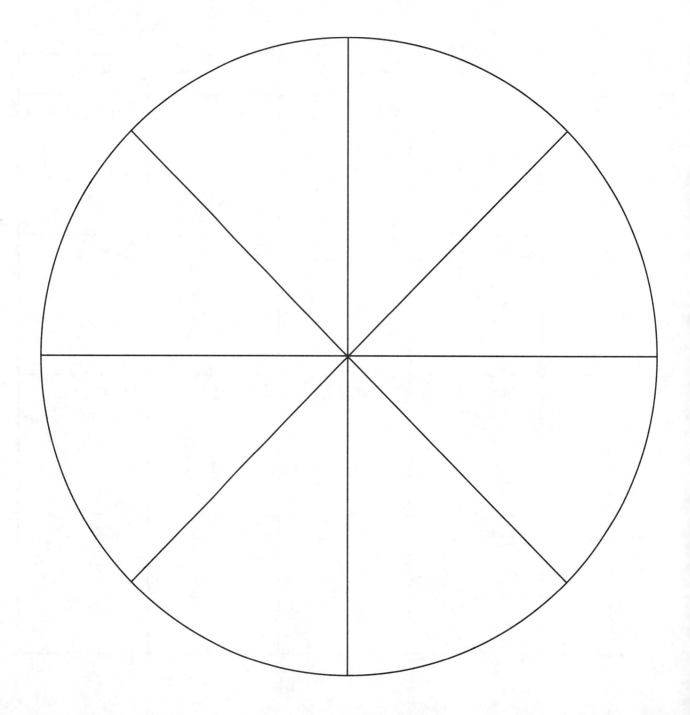

Spelling Squares Contract

Follow these steps to complete your spelling contract:

1. Choose three activities that make a winning tic-tac-toe row, either vertically, horizontally, or diagonally.

2. Use your spelling words to complete each activity.

3. Check off each activity as you complete it.

4. Turn in this Spelling Squares Contract with the final spelling activity.

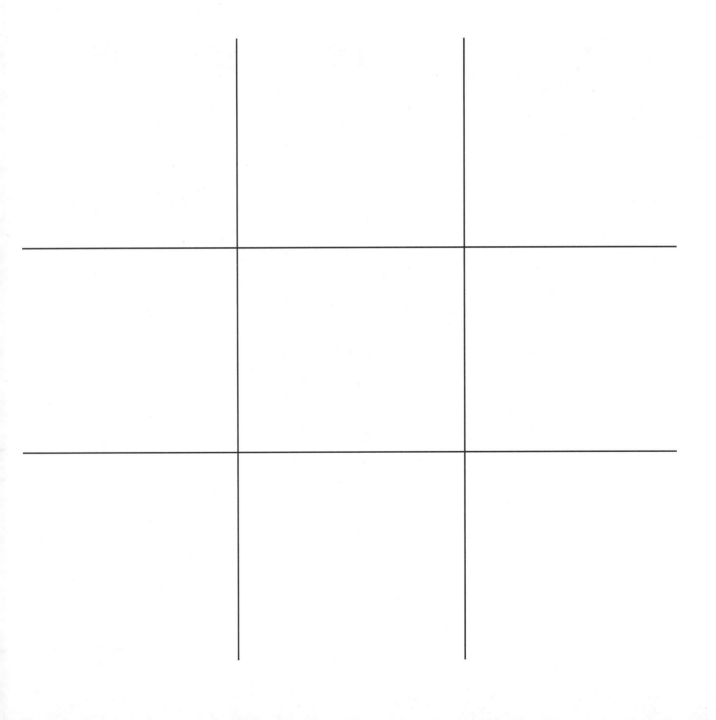

Bingo Contract

Follow these steps to complete your spelling contract:

1. Choose activities that make a winning bingo row, either vertically, horizontally, or diagonally.

2. Use your spelling words to complete each activity.

3. Check off each activity as your complete it.

4. Turn in this Bingo Contract with the final spelling activity.

B I N G O

		FREE SPACE		